Winter Be My Bride

Laura deLeon

Published by

2013

Winter be my Bride by Laura DeLeon

Published by: In Our Words Inc.
             www.inourwords.ca

Editor: Brandon Pitts

Cover image: 'The Annunciation' by
               Dante Gabriel Rossetti
               dated 1850

Author Photo: Brandon Pitts

Book design: Shirley Aguinaldo

Library and Archives Canada Cataloguing in Publication

DeLeon, Laura, author
        Winter be my bride : poems / Laura DeLeon.

ISBN 978-1-926926-29-2 (pbk.)

        I. Title.

PS8607.E48275W56 2013   C811'.6   C2013-902436-0

'Narcissus and Lady of the Lake,' previously published in *Angels In Twilight*, Beret Days Press, TOPS, January, 2010

'Lady of the Lake,' previously published in *Spirit Eyes and Fireflies, An Anthology*, Beret Days Press, TOPS, September 2011

'Forever and Ever and In Bliss,' originally published in *Ropedancer, An Anthology*, Beret Days Press, TOPS, August 2012

'My Chai and The Mind's Eye,' previously published in *The Verse Afire*, by TOPS.

All Rights Reserved. Copyright ©Laura DeLeon, 2013. The author retains all rights to the contents of this book. Brief quotes may be used with source credit.

DEDICATION

I lovingly dedicate this book to the memory
of my departed grandfather
Rudolph Stafford DeLeon,
better known to everyone
as 'Rudy'

TABLE OF CONTENTS

Introduction.. 6
I Am My Father's Soul 8
Keep Pure, Sleep With The Angels 9
Narcissus... 10
Echo.. 11
Lady Of The Lake 12
Ophelia's Death.. 13
Like A Broken-Wing Bird 15
Emily Dickinson 16
My Chai 17
A Faint Rainbow 18
An Alignment Of Shadows 19
Orbs Of Light... 20
An Awakening From...................................... 21
A Dream.. 21
A Future Poem.. 22
Desire Of My Heart, ... 23
Beloved Of My Soul 23
Euphoric Ode To Spiritual Love 25
Should A Tear Fall... 26
Peace Is The Most Treasured Thing On Earth........... 27
Forever And Ever 28
In Bliss.. 29
Precipice 30
Patience 31
Cajun.. 32
Spirit Of The Tree 33
Spring Revisited 34
Love Friendly 35
The Grapevine 36
Lit... 36
Satin Wing Tip.. 37
Hand 38
Thus Far 39
Peace 40
I Beat The System 41
Weakness Of The Flesh................................... 42

TABLE OF CONTENTS

The Deed 43
Dread Goddess 44
Babylon 45
The Mast 46
Perfect Attraction 47
Spiritual Bliss 48
Euphoria 49
Day Of The Dead 50
Be Mine 51
Change 52
Moonlight 53
The Lost Love Of Juliet 54
Marlene Dietrich 56
Bella Luna 57
Advance 58
Your Request 59
Pure 60
The Darkness 61
Disarming 62
One World 63
Love Is The Answer 64
Farewell 65
Graveyard Years 66
Winter Be My Bride 67
Meadows 68
Humanity Descends 68
Night Shade 69
In The Sphere Of Love 70
The Minds Eye 71
These Three Wishes 72
Open Wound 74
From The Grave 75
Purge 76
Safe 77
The Garden 78
Acknowledgments 80

INTRODUCTION

I am living proof that there are angels in our midst. For if it had not been for the existence of angels I would not be where I am today. My belief and love of angels is two-fold. First and foremost, from a very early age, or perhaps even before I was born into this world, my mother surrounded me with beautiful art, music and literature to feed the soul.

Secondly, my father had a talent for writing poetry. He won first prize for lyrical poetry in the West Indies before graduating high school and immigrating to Canada.

I have come to honor my parents, Carol and Alton DeLeon for having given me the gift of life and encouraging me in all of my endeavors. I am eternally grateful for their love and support, encouragement and their dedication to 50 years of marriage. I am humbled and honored to follow in their footsteps and to be the receptacle of their love.

My writings have been influenced by the mystical muse of the lover and the immortal Beloved, similar to the fabled love poem *'The Prophet'* by Khalil Gibran. Peace and love are two themes that are one and the same within the genre of Sufi poetry. My poems reflect flights of fancy and resonate themes of romantic idealism. Conjured in free verse or rhyme they divine meaning from the nocturnal, the spiritual and the sublime in nature. It took heart and soul to write these poems from a place of spiritual solace. My belief in and reliance on transcendentalism also helped bring these poems into light.

I am proud to say I have made the giant leap of faith from writing poetry and free verse to emerging as a voice in the poetry community and performing my poetry for reading and listening audiences alike. It is my sincere hope that these poems resound true to the mystical experience and impress upon the reader that angelic encounters do exist and that there are angels in our midst.

Laura DeLeon
June 2013

I Am My Father's Soul

i am my father's soul
once a fisherman of the deep
tranquil oceans and the seas
erupting violent storm

teach us of waves crashing
teach us to be still
among the craggy hills
and rocks
teach us to listen
to the siren of the seas

let us watch the water
glisten pure and pristine
among the wavering
shores of time
let us divine spirits
from sweet waters

let us not drown our souls
in sadness and despair
let us pray for truth
let us have faith in our prayers

KEEP PURE, SLEEP WITH THE ANGELS

Now I lay me down to die
I pray that sleep will come soon
With weary bones I shut mine eyes
Yet on this precipice, this holy arc
Angels arrive at my tomb, unharmed
I arise to meet my maker
And to behold of the dream
I am the dreamer
The one to walk among the living
Now deceased
The ancient being calleth me to sleep
I adhere to the calling
For this is my one divine night
By divine right
My heart in exultation
To be among the stars
And the visionaries within
Into the arms of the universe

NARCISSUS

How much are these wishes?
What are they worth in tears?
Do they reach you
from here to
the bottom of the lake?
Do they resonate
like songs murmured
word for word,
across the bay,
to the evergreens
in the misty morning?

Visions of sylphs and fays
run wild and stray, then
return to the place
that was luminous
and deep

Keep your promise fallen angel
I will call unto you
to the world of dreams
beyond the depths
of your subconscious state

I will find you
in perfect form
the mirror reflection
will draw you in, and
return you unto me

ECHO

perchance one wish will find you
at the innermost part
at your innermost peace
at the bottom of the sea
of darkening, an epiphany
your lost years—and lost time
awakening to the tide
laid to rest: I am your reflection
spotless, speckless and perfect
in perfection
now given a second sense
a renewed purpose of life
like water distilled in a glass
divining spirits from the lake
uncoiling, recoiling, free-falling
free of fear: I am your reflection
the innermost spirit of the years
set adrift on the internal spheres
of nurturing and motherhood
you had no place
sucked inside the deep vortex
between time and space
a perpetual disillusion
forevermore and forever after
the displacement of all time
the sign of the contract
the way to counteract
and avoid another vicious attack
perchance you will find me
all dressed in black
for I am your reflection

LADY OF THE LAKE

Sweet Ophelia
why must thou go
fair maid
when all that remains
are fragments
of a delusion?

Be at peace
with thy keepsakes

Sleep as a mermaid
among the lilies
and the leaves
away from the
deathly pale
cold heart of stone

The art of one mind
the purpose of one soul
exists from within
the chambers of thy heart
reciting poetry and song
seeking shelter

Belong to the trees
in thy secret world

OPHELIA'S DEATH

Sweet girl, sacrosanct, one love
to thee,
Far be it for me to call you away
from thy attrition,
an act of love,
life's chosen course
to make amend of things
gone horribly wrong.

Sleep in peace, be at rest,
God rest thy soul
in true comfort
and manifold bounties
and blessings.
Lo and behold,
be blessed.

May heaven's dressings find thee
in perfect clandestine
mon ange, my queen
betrothed to remain unseen.

To be at one
with the jaded Sun
The one whom they call
the divine naysayer
the fateful slayer
the remover of all sin.

What is done is done.
Nay, may all things
be blessed,
be laid to rest.

The chosen one
Sweet Ophelia,
Lady of the Lake,
who is now deceased.
Be at rest, sleep in peace.

LIKE A BROKEN-WING BIRD

like a broken-wing bird
I lapse between one world
and another

forever beseeching flight
into the dark of night
of the world of dreams
yet never quite arriving
at my place in the sun

I ascend on the wings of a prayer
hoping you are there
to find me well within your reach
having once seen your celestial being
knowing that you still honour
our life in the clouds
in bliss and love through our sacred oath

EMILY DICKINSON
775 EFFIGIES

recovery on the wings of prayer
silken threads and silver strings
I mend your angel wings with care
in all your resplendent finery
no one has ever burned brighter
so close to the flame
as a moth is drawn into firelight
satin divinity with each
and every stitch
fine outstretched
in fragile frame
in a web-like maze
transformation is at hand
a spindle spun and woven
to the imagination
set fire to your flame
a vision in flight
a dream in white light
a life's work
though not in vain

MY CHAI

You are the unicorn
that held the glass to my eyes
You gave me sight
faith in the open hand
I cried myself to sleep silently in your arms
at one with the dead of night
The songs you cradled me in
invoked poetry and spoke of dreams

You are the storm
my tempest in a teapot
the earth beneath my feet

breaking ground . . . I am found
and no more a lost soul
Sifting through the sands
I levitate and am one
with white light

Forever luminous
at the heart of darkness
quickened
at the moment of truth
a deluge to endure
a slow death and afterlife
drawing breaths from vapours
the sweetness I savour

A Faint Rainbow

We are the tainted glass
The windows of your soul
Cut into pieces
Divisions of light
Fragments of a whole
Transparent,
Invisible to the sun
Fragile,
Not frail,
Yet delicate.

Protect us,
For we are your visions,
Your waves
And your quest
No more shy of reality
Than the rays of the sun
A child of creation
A daughter of the universe
A divine revelation.

An Alignment of Shadows

The night is catching
up with the sun

In fervor and defiance
all is one

The moon in levitation
and orbital essence

in perfect alignment
looking down
on humanity
from above

The stars in rotation
have fallen from the sky

mine eyes have seen you cry
tears of angels
on the wings of a dove

ORBS OF LIGHT

Transcendental flowers in bloom
at the heavenly gate of your garden
at the heart of your graven tomb

I am humbled
my footsteps hesitant
as I enter
your sacred garden

I find myself conscious
in a state of awareness
a blissful awakening
to the rites of spring
a marriage of the mind
the body and soul

In your field of pure gold
I long for this moment
to capture in my hands
and give it to you

crystal orbs of light
visions of clear blue

An Awakening from a Dream

(In memory of Irving Layton)

Awaiting your ship to sail
I lay awake at night
in a state of ordinance
and bliss

Reel in your lost Beloved
of the seas
and I promise
you shall not grieve, nor bereave
for lost time

Mine eyes have singled you out
a world sequestered
unto yourself

The path you have chosen
the light that you follow
the home that you will call
your very own

"Like a vampire's wing, the stillness in dead feet,"
waiting in your wings, I am anxious
whilst I wax and wane
knowing of a true love
that once was lost
nothing now appears in vain

No wasted attempt at life or death

The dirge song that lingers on
the siren state of dreaming

A Future Poem

just a precipice
an entanglement
of estranged angels
overlooking their
judgment day

permit me to say
i was only chasing rainbows

Desire of My Heart, Beloved of My Soul

I fell on dark days, quite innocently
I fled for refuge from that place
I perish the thought
of ever looking back

I embarked upon a journey
dancing on a dark night of the soul

In a desolate graveyard
I followed my heart
and remained until
the end of time

It was there I thought
I could find peace of mind
a place to rest and retreat
into utter nothingness

It was one divine night
all my dreams crystallized
came to life
like a prayer wheel in motion

Angels in ecstasy watched over me
raised my spirit aloft in time
A raven's eye, a dove's sigh
to hold the tears in
guiding me into the arms
of my Beloved kin

As blessings from above
fill my heart with love
and deliver my soul
with the light from within
    the darkness that subsides

EUPHORIC ODE TO SPIRITUAL LOVE

The soul subsides between black and grey
Re-emerges from the shadows into the blue
One shade more dark, beneath sunlit rays
More sustained, a deeper hue
Purple sunlight's candour sways
Even the most reticent of fools
Old age is now discretely played
By the young at heart whose love is true
What faith, what force is that of mind
Whose powers are far greater than one's will
Waves and currents, dreams divine
Euphoric odes of love fulfilled
Mystic man of love sublime
Of the pure and magical
Stars that dwell in heaven's climb
Thy ancient heart, Thy sovereign will

Should A Tear Fall

Brighten my eyes, kindly align with me
In my darkest hour, be kind to me
As I gazed upon the brightest star in the sky
A teardrop welled within my eye
Though I did not cry, by thy gentle grace
I looked to find a sacred place
In among the forest and the trees
Holding fast and true unto a leaf
I took my seat on the mossy green
Where by chance I found a stream
And thereupon the forest floor
Were the prayers and thoughts of my heart's core
In all that is one with the world and at peace
I should hope this feeling shall never cease

PEACE IS THE MOST TREASURED THING ON EARTH

You don't seem to take direction well
The first time I tried to show you kindness
You were ambivalent towards me
You walked away from the unforeseen calamity
Untouched.

When I tried to tell you of my dreams
You would not listen
Each one bearing manifold bounty and blessing
With you at the centre.

If I could paint a picture with my tears
Of remorse, regret and longing,
Could I turn you around?
Could I catch a glimpse of a moment
Before it passes and hold it in my hands?

If I reach out to you again
Before this world ends
Will you turn away from me
Or would you welcome me into your arms?

FOREVER AND EVER

Love, you were loved
in a past life.
Fast asleep you are now.
Blessed angels follow you.
In nightly visions,
appear to you in dreams.

Poetic bliss upon pure lips,
the substance of the ephemeral
and the last in passing.
Enigmatic, ingénue
how did it fly with you,
beautiful?

I cried by the wayside.
Wild flowers with you
diffuse holy fragrance at night
in the colour of your dreams.

IN BLISS

I cover your darkness
across the streets
blinded by your beauty
in the light of day
homespun in my spinning yarn

unravel with me my love
in a web of dreams before us

your countenance
pure and silver
your willingness
your heart and abode

the streaming clouds above
prevail, full of promise

Paint the sky with your tears
distilled for a moment
in harm's way

reflecting the rays of the sun
catching luminous days undone

PRECIPICE

then leave this quiet place
the same way you found it
the stars above
weeping down on you
just leave
and free this space on earth

entranced in the moment
from darkness into light
you are my star
my brilliant future ahead
will you be the one
to see me through this

cryptic illusionist
magician of the dark
I kiss your lips . . . blue
turned black
I am revived and returned
back to life

PATIENCE

In an empty room of whispering wounds
The science of walls and floor tiles
The inevitable silences
Sitting on stones
Resting in alms

Speech is prayer
Irreverent thereafter
At random order and in tandem
Seeing oneself in side-long glances
Through the fountain, a waterfall mirror
Of the unseen

At the corner of the eye
Denotations of light and dark
Flights and frenzies, flutter by
Little glimmer, glistening
In a fevered fire of lost energy
Revealing itself
Inertia

Peace is at the heart
Of this deep water well
Sanguine and red
Consecrated, spirited
From out of the woodwork
One by one, we come
Fractured at the bone
Still inclined to morph
Into being and linger
In languid movement

CAJUN

the cracking, the crushing
the breaking of bones
under the wailing wind

alone . . . . the silent tears
gathering at the threshold
to be caged from within
is the silence
like a Cajun tiger trapped
inside its own stripes
afraid of its own shadow

out of its element
like a prized possession
in a gilded cage
or a window display case
the on-rushers and passers by
leer and jeer

nothing catching to the eye
the universal mind has died
this guiding force
this carriage without a horse
life must carry onward

Spirit of the Tree

Images that transcend space and time
Inhabit a place within my mind
Satiated for a moment clear
Trust in faith, the soul shall appear
No more imperceptive to the light
A captive to the celestial flight
A happenstance of Fortune's grace
Profound understanding of one's place
Upon the sweet geneal base of the tree
Spring forth, branch out in ecstasy
Into visions of other worlds divine
A mirror image to the mind
Outward expression, the clay of thought
Of that which of the soul hath wrought
Moulding and sculpting, time exists in temperance
Alas, I know of a certain frame of reference
That exists solely in and of desire
Enkindled in love flamed passion's fire
Cradled in the arms of angel wings
This place where I have heard the spirit sing

Spring Revisited

Cherry blossom in the dead of winter
Reveals itself in the rite of spring
Summer calling in distant voices
The earth's sacred offering

Pure unaltered as the air
The birds have left the branches bare
Threads upon the trees, an angel's nest
All God's creatures laid to rest

The site of spring through the looking glass
Dew dropped kisses upon the grass
Blessed renewal of old love vows
Birds that sing upon the boughs
Breathing in new life, welcoming new love
An adoration of spirits and kindred
Spirit creatures . . . of the kingdom above

LOVE FRIENDLY

I lost track of my kin
And my folk
I played the game
My heart like a flame of fire
In the darkest night
I arose from my slumber
To seek out my loved ones
My best Beloved

Dispassionate love flame
I hold no blame
For thou art thine heart
I love thee just the same

Emblazon my name
upon thy heart
Set fire to the flame
If truly thou art
Set then our feet firm
On the same parallel plane
So we may not be consumed
So that we may recommence
Resume and begin again

Through and through

THE GRAPEVINE

crushing the grapes
into wine
fruit of the vine
how bitter the taste
this forbidden fruit
yet choice among the gods
remains a sacrament

LIT

a sunset plateau
a vanishing point
that highlights the sky
of pink iridescence
climbing towards heavens high
a stairway of obeisance

Satin Wing Tip

moon gazing moths
appear like prayers
released into the atmosphere
from the underworld
moving spellbound
and freely
white winged luminosity
central to their nocturnal
nature
an outward escapism
flights of fancy
and self-preservation
in the spirit world

in a fleeting moment
the scattering of pollen
dust
silken flowers
released into the atmosphere
cinder love flowers of the night

HAND

take my hand
the inner life of the spirit
the eyes to the soul
the mind's eye
that reaches outward
toward the core
in your angelhood

where the innocence
resides
teardrops from your eyes
that shine
illumined in the darkness

an outpouring of secret love
that never ceases to amaze
in this still moment in time
I dance this wave through
to the very end of your sojourn
and your stay here
in the kingdom of heaven
above

THUS FAR

are we merely parts
the sum of a whole?
a fatal oppression
that plays itself out
each time we attempt
to reconcile
with good intention
to join the pieces
together
like a composition
of lost time
an art to the mind
to acknowledge matters of the heart
will our souls
inevitably be
one extension of another?
joined and pieced
together
in perfect harmony?

PEACE

Tear your veils asunder
Walk through the kingdom of shadows
Cry bitter tears of remorse
Be in the guise of gods

In the name of the bearer of fruit
Mother goddess seeking child
All the while betrothed to the fire
Of Hades

Take this elixir
Charm and remedy
This fragrant incense
And you will be granted immortality
And given back your light and life

I Beat the System

i was once an angry man
before i made peace
with the gods of war
and settled the score

in this dispensation
i am one
the Bacchae sun
cannot change me

Dionysus will then feed me
with a silver spoon
with which i will partake of
this heavenly feast

my ear to the ground
my eye to the sky
suddenly am i
an avenger
to a savage cruel world?

WEAKNESS OF THE FLESH

two lovers torn apart
at the threshold
before the kingdom
of heaven
the chalice of their devotion
left to fate alone
immersed in the stream
of divine utterance
redeemed, washed clean
the stain
then turned to stone
the call of the Beloved
the taking of vows
to follow under oath
in spiritual union
betrothed
the purple garment
the colour of dreams
to come

THE DEED

Pomegranate . . . seed of life and death
Taste of forbidden fruit to the test
Summoned in the name of Zeus
An act of gentle persuasion
A mother's love and indignation
Raised from the barren earth
A fragile state in question and unrest
Threatening the life of other tribes
Gods, immortals
Demeter, teacher of sacred rites,
Will you till the soil again?
Will your daughter be returned unto you
When the dark soul of the underworld
Shall find it in his heart
To relieve Persephone from captivity
When the earth shall be restored
And all things renewed?

DREAD GODDESS

unmarred by time
a gathering of souls immortal
she rides the waves
a flower among friends
a hundred blossoms
perfume petals
and roses in bloom
sweet neurosis
nocturnal flowers
in the sea of light
laughter crashing in waves
drawn into the deep
the earth's gaping hole
seized by the underground
world of Hades
maiden to bride
none to perceive
to hear her cries
a stranger to the new world

BABYLON

In the temple garden of paradise
The planting of the Tree of Life
The sowing of the seed

Snake at the roots
Bird in the branches

Lilith joins and marries
The heir to the underworld
In sacred union

Wishing for her bed
A throne
All creatures
Take leave of the tree

Gods and Goddess
Reclaimed, alone

THE MAST

born under the deadly sign
of cancer
water, moonshine and the tides
perhaps i should change my name
or become a poet just the same
start a fire, set fire to my flame
spit fire
and throw flames at the sky
catapult . . . on a deadly high
scatter ashes to the ground
confound
the deep among us
in amazement
to live no more in abasement
a shower of petals at their feet
smashing idols on the street
your precious words, so sweet
endearing
precarious to me, my dear one
i harbour no envy
just your love flame
just a world of regret
just the same
i have put the past behind
choosing never to look back
casting a blind eye
to the masses unkind

PERFECT ATTRACTION

you kissed in perfection
I behold your beauty
beyond the phases of the moon
you found me as you found
Venus orbiting
around you
witnessed a truth
known to only you
an unknowable essence

now a life dispossessed
of feeling
is a life devoid of meaning
only crime and punishment
discontent
all the good in the world
is of no consequence

a time to atone
a perfect cut stone
a diamond in the rough
at the end of the road
paved with gold
and good intention
that rises to meet you
with no deception or hatred
no dead-end track, no remorse
no break in the continuity
just mind and depth
coming up for air

Spiritual Bliss

testing the waters
i fear in bliss
may not be too deep
this tryst for diving
in spiritual solace
a God-given gift
the palm of the right hand
held close
to near death
experience this
experimental
the elusive kiss
never before engendered
unto one's self
the joy of hyperbolic
juvenilia, synesthesia
a death-defying act
walking the tightrope
of reason, defiance
and restraint
unadulterated and pure
the evanescence of truth
untold and revered

EUPHORIA

There is a certain sadness
about you, my love,
something in your eyes.

A Delphic oracle
you and I enmeshed
in this tryst.

Synthesized to the
outermost limits
of this inner peace.

Isolationist terminal
change of address
your installation
my heart's desire.

Tear-stained madness
of love in distress
by the hands of the clock
I will not tire.

Locked into the hour of darkness
and desire, the fire burning
sanitation of hands and mind
the true revelation of
conscience kind.

DAY OF THE DEAD

my porcelain skin
my camouflage complexion
your ashen pallor
your sin i suffer
your thorny disposition
lo and behold
thou art my heart
the rose that i adorn
who truly thou art?
a rose among thorns
a garland halo
around my head
to be worn
on that precise
precipitous day
the day of the dead
and all soul's night
and the witching hour
that commences
whereby the primordial
spirit shall be set free
manifest itself
into the world of being
and I shall mend
thy wicked ways

BE MINE

fraught with hatred
distraught but kind
touch me not
for my beating heart
is no longer blind

may i linger into
other worlds sublime?
i was locked into
an undead world
i came to you
an absolute truth
an airborne spirit
in flight, untouched by time

i was looked to
as a wounded dove
not a stranger in love
but a songbird of nigh

i had made your acquaintance
as i had prayed once before
as i had clearly seen the sign

your cinder love flowers
i adore, your spirit invocations
i speak your praises in rhyme
i beseech the sun's rays to be kind
in accordance with
your conscious mind

i am at one, i am fine.
i feel your Memnoch breeze
your heart deceased
for true love
i shall not cast away
for i loved you
the very first day that i found you
leaving no trace
of the past gone by behind

my love and my heart
is with you all the time
no schisms
to cloud the mind
just pure adulation, reverberation, reciprocation
for this heart of mine

CHANGE

the changing of times
the caging of minds
carry forward and follow through

the changing of minds
the effacement of time
soaring . . . flying . . . taking to the air
tether to your self
to thine own self be true

MOONLIGHT

are we of the moon
like lunar creatures of the night?

unearthed emerging from twilight to dusk
the unhinged spirit sings
conjuring divination
a divine revelation
the solstice incantation

like grains of sand
the passing time
configurations
time signatures
in the muse of listening
attuned to the soul
as angels and their wings
thus cosmic retribution
the spirit of all things
luminosity, illumined

THE LOST LOVE OF JULIET

Not a hospice for the sick
A place for the dying young

We lay love down in the trenches
Until our time hath come

Let us begin again
Sow the seed in fields where we lay

Our moonlight vigil
To the nightingale of truth we pray

He who cannot be preyed upon
For love is greater than sighs

And tears and futile cares
My star . . . my treasure . . . my prize

The power of sadness
At the hour of death

The dying hour
I lie asleep at thy breast

In thy sacred trust
If God's love lay dying

Then the deceased we shall be
And we must

And the dead we are
No feet to tread upon the earth

Made of dust, drenched in
Jasmine, rose petals, tea leaves and musk

No not dead, nay merely asleep
Having ingested the poison deep

I drank to thee well within
Hence came sleep

In close company I keep
And cherish thine heart

Die, at once my love
So soon we shall depart

MARLENE DIETRICH

Your sweet lips
Your incandescence
Your graven image haunts me
Still there is love to be seen
Well be it with you, within your heart
Be true, evangelical
Angel eyes
Spark of light
That mystery
That shining beauty
On the silver screen
O to be adored
Sanctified and appraised
Beyond the realist truth
And of divine nature
Mon martre and the sages
Deviant yet unrequited
Unembellished, yet brilliant
You light up the screen
With your fire and ice
Love be it with a vengeance

Bella Luna

Serpentine recoil
Passion flower
Butterfly blossom
Lotus petals

Soul bathed in light
Am I the one in love with the Sun?
Does anyone see the Sky?

Not blind to the sight
Yet pinned down
Held against your will
Broken in
Wings singed

You are an innocent by right
Burdened by kindness
A spirit in their midst
Open to the naked eye

They cannot feel your plight
Nor focus on your pillar of light
Acknowledge your brightness

A spiritual rite
A passage obscured
From one portal of light
To another

Advance

head over heels
love at first sight
a chance meeting
of true minds
and souls that transcend
other borders in time
traversing the sky
fine intuition
darkness descends
upon high and low
taking hold of my soul
keeping time
with every step
congruent
the spirit life
slowly advances away
from my heart
like veils burnt asunder
and torn apart

YOUR REQUEST

The tree of life is sapped of sweetness
The tree of knowledge remains
I reap what you sow
quintessential, yet above all else
divine

Your request
how beautiful and strange
The mystic nightingale of paradise
embodies your blessed being
asking to be led to the promised one
seeking peace, a promise to be made
unconstrained and everlasting
delivered from one world
to the next

PURE

o nature's metaphysician!
o divine oracle!
the poetic voice that is echoed
throughout the highs and lows
of this shallow existence
have we fallen off our course
of dreams without fruition?
the soul is a dark horse
a fleeting shadow in the night

THE DARKNESS

lilies distilled in tears
unwelcome ghosts
unpleasant fears

seeping through the sieve
find their way
into the utter darkness

the disease of deception
is alive and well

tears that tear
through the silences
a respite for the soul

skeletons in the closet
await their consolation
for years of complacency
and apathetic intervention

there is no more hope
within this wishing well
no reason to dwell
within the darkness of despair

DISARMING

photographs lost in the fire
the trappings of the mind
soul in seclusion
confined to another life
unadulterated

take away these razor sharp things
and hide them in a box
filled with remnants
of miscellaneous dreams
and lost hope

a paradox
the kind of blind faith
in humanity
is like trying to restore life
to a broken-winged bird
fallen from the nest

ONE WORLD

head over heels one may say
deeper, further into the abyss
the dark void
the black hole matrix
of an underworld existence
to find freedom in nothingness
and disparate distress
arbitrary involvement
and disconnectedness
no chaos from the world alone
can alter this
transcendence our only hope
to rise above the matrix
of moral chaos
to take the next step
toward our common ground
our terra firma
our brave new world awaits

LOVE IS THE ANSWER

Shall I relinquish my light
A star to your sky
In the illimitable space and atmosphere
From the retreats on high
Your universe, a guiding force
Unto my world, undulating tide

I shall not fear the fate of ever-after
And forevermore

Weep not for the past and the duration of lost years
Perpetual grace and infinite blessings be upon you

My dear,
Forget me not, for I am here
In transcendent presence beyond a doubt
Elysian draws us nearer
Within love and without

FAREWELL

This is healing
Incessant, revealing
Surfacing, latent, immanent
Granted impart from the retreats on high
What nature hath intended to be
To redeem and circumvent
That which is eminent
The excess of self-indulgence
Pure and stringent
A time to medicate and slough away
With no trials to be had
No misgivings, delusions
This is disillusionment
Hell-bent on morality
Just inner strength
And more power
Toward the core
The very spirit of life
From within
That now lies dormant
Death wishes us all farewell

GRAVEYARD YEARS

hey, are you digging my gold mine?
souls do pray and linger on
for some time
gold diggers and skullduggery
the order of the day
are you not reading correctly the sun?
perhaps that is why
the planets have not aligned
and the stars are not favourable signs

such a shame and pity
that this must be the fate
of all who were young
now laid to rest
and gone to dust
triumphant as it seemed
it was just a dream

the decaying and depravity
of breaking down
the eye that fails to see
the truth for itself
flowers uprooted and strewn
at your feet
books burned and thrown
off the shelf
milkweed, goldenrod, Queen Anne's lace
wilder than the wildest dream
or landscape within itself
must these prayers go unanswered
these tablets revealed yet, unsung?

WINTER BE MY BRIDE

Take my hand and learn my love
Frozen in time, so below and all above
Walk in my way, in the tyranny of our lives
Kiss mine eyes my Beloved
So that I may see the way, within and without
Forlorn
I have the thorn in my hand
You wear the crown
I carry the roses, my love, my Beloved
Goddess to priest of the underground
Betrothed to death from above, he saith

Why are hearts made of stone?
Why are souls lost in ruin?

MEADOWS

rivers meandering and flow
tributary unwind divine
currents of the mind
places of the soul

to unravel and follow
your heart and soul
to adhere and behold
traces of another kingdom
way down below
time to rivet and follow
follow, follow
let the river flow

HUMANITY DESCENDS

Woman created in the image of God
Equal to man
The subordination of Eve
Daughter to Adam
Removed from Mother Goddess
Obliterated, eliminated
Humanity descends

NIGHT SHADE

Shimmering leaves in the dead of night
Awaken to the shade of dreams
Coloured and drenched in pale moonlight
Wrapped in gauze and velveteen
Bloodlet roses of delight
Travel beneath the silent stream
Painted flowers of spiral skies
Dripping jewels of cherubim
Images flashing through my mind
At the speed of evanescent beam
Thoughts disperse into twilight
Unfold the ever-present dream
Merge into the morning light
Revisiting magical mystical scenes
Through the veil of visionary sight
Behold the truth of inner meaning

IN THE SPHERE OF LOVE

Wipe the tears from mine eyes
Build me up from the clay and mire
Raise me from the water and sand

Bewitching and enchanted,
I was called into being
my metamorphoses,
to the seas open wide
and the sands of time

Awaiting the relentless tide
on the shores of distant dreams

A mermaid of the mist
unveils her raven locks
sitting upon the rocks
she is singing her siren song
calling out to her Beloved

In the spur of the moment
the air is pure
filled with rain and incense
of good and true intent

THE MINDS EYE

the first light to spark
and ignite the fire
under the eye
of loving kindness
and in the arms
of sweet delivery
cradled beneath
the deep solitary mind.

I embrace this elusive moment
reciprocal in space
never to lose sight
or fade away.

locked in memory
channeled in energy
feeds the fire and inspire
my dream to light.

THESE THREE WISHES

I fly your colours
Dynamite . . . I dance with you
On other flights of fancy
I give my hell to you . . . in disguise
And in discretion and wise
Who will fill these shoes
That were made for you?

Who will see me through
This tragic fall
Into life and love

Who will brush off
This mortal dust?
When in bloom
These cinder flowers
Shall rise to the occasion
And shall not be consumed
To be left in ruin

Who will release the dove?
Must I fear the reaper?
All of this doom and gloom
Surely I have had enough of
This near death
To live and die out of love?

I have this thing called dying
Down to an art
To live and die for love
In this remote place
This romantic suicide

This diminutive soul
This dying race
What have I left to give?
With all the answers
To the questions
Will the universe provide?

Let not this water well
Run dry
Dipping into my pool
Of dreams
And visions unseen
To the naked eye

OPEN WOUND

the scars on my feet
don't lie
in ancient times
they were ruins
sweet telepathy
and alchemy
imminent wounds
on the high rise

it pains me
to see you
to feel you
this way
my gift of faith
is as much a detriment
to me as it is an attribute
the cause of much pain
and heartache

this talent that has
cut my heart out
and tears right through
my own psyche

of this I do reprove of
stone cold and drunk
on love...

FROM THE GRAVE

Cumulative clouds prevailing
Now it is time to open your eyes
Shadows shift in paradigm
Sift through space and time
Other states of consciousness
Awareness of the mind

A storm is immanent
In plain view
Pressing, making its way
Through the firmament
Unapologetic

Thoughts that stray into
Stream of consciousness
Awakened by a ray of light
Un-condescending, relative,
Free-flowing,
Divine in nature
Of the sublime

Into the clear blue
Ice crystal formations
Paint the scene
The outer framework
Of the innermost being

PURGE

You parted the sea
You walked the wind
Like footsteps in the sand
You are the waves

To the sandstone I abide
Your hands reach out
To the ends of the earth
My perception changes
As time marches onward
The mind reflects in candor
All is calm beneath the waves

Truth has been established
Prayers of true faith
Shall come to fruition
Quickened through the fire
Our love shall not perish
Yet stand the test of time

SAFE

no need to be startled by the winds of change
crashing violent waves of destruction, a disruption
of the peace and tranquillity, the moss and peat
thrashing about the stones, a deadly storm
water rising to dangerous heights and frightening feats

just leave the tempest at bay
the lost will find their way
try to find something real, tactile, tangible
to hold on to for dear life
try to resist the urge
to be carried away and pulled under with the tide
the deep dark sea presents a bride
a mermaid in her midst

THE GARDEN

If it were that we met
In the past
In a past life
One moment in time
The time of our life
Ours would be the kingdom
The kingdom of God
And heaven above
The kingdom of God's love
Would be thine
For we would not thirst
Nor rehearse
A passion's play
A bitter tale
After blood or lust
We would partake
Of the fruit of the branch
Of the Tree of Life
And live in our own regard
And sacred trust
And feed of our hunger
Without fear or strife
We would live life
To the fullest
And live and survive
Off the fat of the land
Drink from our hands
The very sweetness of milk and honey
Never to be in want of anything
Denied unto man
Subservient unto himself
Ours, our haven would neither be

Heaven nor hell,
Not a manger or a church
Nay, a garden of angels
Paradise on earth
Nothing would be beyond reproach
Together we would live beneath the stars
The sun . . . the moon . . . the universe . . . ours

Acknowledgments

I wish to acknowledge those who have helped make this dream come into fruition: The Ontario Poetry Society and The Gadist Circle. They helped shape me into the poet that I am today. At the top of my list is Bunny Iskov, who helped nurture my talent. I also wish to thank Bunny's father, Jay Charles Hershberg, 'The Golden Poet,' whose soul now rests in peace. His loving kindness and good spirit is a constant source of inspiration as is his poetry. He is another example that angels do exist.

A special word of thanks to my editor and dearest friend in the literary world, Brandon Pitts, for believing in me from the start, helping me hone my craft, perfect my art and for introducing me to other worlds of poetry. Much love and inspiration to you my dear friend. Peace, love and respect to my Gadist kinsmen, Nik Beat and Stedmond Pardy for being instrumental and quintessential to my life and development as a poet. I cannot forget Cheryl Antao-Xavier, my publisher, whose kindness, support and expert advice are invaluable to me. I sent her my precious words and she transformed them into a beautiful array of poems. I would also like to thank my parents for angelic visions and goodly deeds shared with me on a daily basis. Their wish is that my life be blessed and fulfilled with peace, love, joy and happiness garnered over the years.

And last but not least I thank God for granting me the gift of serenity and the opportunity to share this message with others.

Peace, love and harmony.

Laura

www.ingramcontent.com/pod-product-compliance
Lightning Source LLC
Chambersburg PA
CBHW071539080526
44588CB00011B/1728